The Educator's Quotebook

Topically Arranged

compiled by Edgar Dale

A Publication of the Phi Delta Kappa
Educational Foundation
Bloomington, Indiana

cover design by Nancy Rinehart

Library of Congress Catalog Card Number 83-63095
ISBN 0-87367-429-4
Foreword copyrighted © 1984 by the
Phi Delta Kappa Educational Foundation
Bloomington, Indiana

Acknowledgements

I wish to acknowledge the help on *The Educator's Quotebook* that I received over the years from my two co-workers, Joseph O'Rourke and Elizabeth Chapin. These quotations went through their hands at least twice. Further, I want to give credit to Derek L. Burleson, editor of Special Publications at Phi Delta Kappa, for his assistance in classifying and structuring this material. I hope that the time we all spent on this publication will be rewarding to the reader and user.

This book is sponsored by Miss Bessie Gabbard, who made a generous contribution toward publication costs. Miss Gabbard is a member of the Ohio State University Chapter and the Broward County Florida Chapter of Phi Delta Kappa, and she is chairperson of the Phi Delta Kappa Educational Foundation Board of Governors.

Topical Listing

Foreword

This book is concerned with communication — the sharing of good ideas. Those who say things best communicate best. The quotations I've chosen are aimed at informing, inspiring, educating, and entertaining. I hope educators will find here apt thoughts to fit their needs.

I hope also that the material I've included will encourage others to begin a personal file of useful and widely applicable ideas to illustrate the points they want to make in writing, speaking, and teaching. Most of us will jot down a good joke or pungent remark in anticipation of using them at an appropriate time in the future, but that isn't enough. These notes must be classified and filed. Thus I have used classifications for this collection of quotes.

Why did I prepare a book like this? What purposes does it serve? Perhaps my experience as a youth in collecting jokes, riddles, and anecdotes may have something to do with it. Two publications stand out here. One of them was *On A Slow Train Through Arkansaw* by Thomas W. Jackson (1903), which introduced me to riddles such as, Why did the duck dive to the bottom of the pool? Answer: For divers reasons. Or, Why did the duck come up to the surface? Answer: For sundry reasons. I also read at that time many of the *Blue Books* put out by Haldane Company. They had such catchy titles as *Bees and Butterflies*.

Perhaps my interest in this kind of material was responsible for my being appointed joke editor in 1915 of *The Paulsonian*, the Rugby, North Dakota, high school annual. I wrote such nifties as: Why is Harold (a student) like a furnace? Answer: Because all day he smokes and at night he goes out.

Early in my career I was concerned about the difference between training and education. I was introduced to John Dewey's *Democracy and Education* (1916) in a correspondence course I took from the

University of North Dakota when I was superintendent of schools in Webster, North Dakota, from 1922-1924. I see now as I turn to *Democracy and Education* that on page 35 Dewey says: "There may be training, but there is no education."

I have often written and spoken about *learning to learn*. Dewey said: "A possibility of continuing progress is opened up by the fact that in learning one act, methods are developed good for use in other situations. Still more important is the fact that the human being acquires a habit of learning. He learns to learn" (p. 54). Sometimes I'm inclined to think that Dewey plagiarized some of my best ideas.

Today everyone is talking about change. As I turn to this classification I get some help from key comments I've heard or read. For example, William James said: "The greatest discovery of my generation is that human beings can alter their lives by altering their attitudes of mind."

Let's suppose I am planning a lecture or article on the future of education. I have quotations on "The Future." Indeed, I have often written and spoken on this topic. One essay in *The News Letter* (January 1966) was titled "Leapfrogging into the Future." Here I wrote: "The great instrument for leapfrogging into the future is education. No basic reforms are possible without it, and with it there is no limit to what man can do."

What we do today influences our future. Milton Caniff, distinguished comic strip artist, once said: "The good old days are now." Tennyson wrote: ". . . Come, my friends. 'Tis not too late to seek a newer world." Shakespeare too offers us wise advice in *Julius Caesar*:

> There is a tide in the affairs of men
> Which, taken at the flood, leads on to fortune:
> Omitted, all the voyage of their life
> Is bound in shallows and in miseries.

Those who refuse to "follow the crowd" have found solace in this quotation of Thoreau:

> If a man does not keep pace with his companions, perhaps it is because he hears a different drummer. Let him step to the music which he hears, however measured or far away.

Like anyone else, I have favorite authors and favorite sayings, many dealing with (as Wordsworth says) the "music of humanity." I especially like Wordsworth's reference to

> . . . that best portion of a good man's life,
> His little, nameless, unremembered acts
> Of kindness and of love.

The reader will note I have included quite a few quotations from Boswell's *Life of Johnson*. Ambrose Bierce satisfied my need for an occasional wisecrack that wasn't funny, but I thought it was penetrating.

We all like and need to be appreciated. William James said, "The deepest principle of human nature is the desire to be appreciated." One of my favorites is by Mark Twain: "I can live for two months on a good compliment."

How will this book help you? First of all, it will save you time. Some of the best ideas of the ages have been gathered together for you. There is a wide range of subject matter. The material is classified and easy to find.

Second, we learn not only by acting and reacting but also by *interacting* with the ideas of others. A good quotation often stimulates good discussion. An apt phrase draws reaction that develops into interaction. Louisa May Alcott says: "Many argue; not many converse."

Third, the significant people deserve to be remembered. We are better for having stored up in our memory what a Lincoln or a Churchill said on a given occasion. Their expressions are often a distillation of complex ideas best remembered in simple phraseology. The quotations we know are a kind of proof of the ideas and ideals we hold and treasure. To write them, rewrite them, and use them is the best way to retain them. Remember, "To have great poets, there must be great audiences, too." (Walt Whitman)

The quotations in this book deal basically with human affairs. I have used many of them as a regular part of my study, writing, and discussion. They are universal enough to be useful to teachers in many fields. Indeed, many of the quotations point up some important ideas on teaching. For example, Shakespeare, commenting on the wordiness of a character in *Love's Labour's Lost* says: "He draweth out the thread of his verbosity finer than the staple of his argument." Shakespeare also addresses the teacher who wants students to read and observe and then observe and read, when he says of Cassius in *Julius Caesar:*

> He reads much;
> He is a great observer, and he looks
> Quite through the deeds of men.

On reading critically, there is Francis Bacon's much admired quotation: "Some books are to be tasted, others to be swallowed, and some few to be chewed and digested." On the rate of reading we have the advice of poet William Walker who says:

Learn to read slow: all other graces
Will follow in their proper places.

Actually we need to encourage varied rates of reading — some fast, some slow. Otherwise we face the danger noted by James Russell Lowell:

A reading-machine, always wound up and going,
He mastered whatever was not worth the knowing.

Some teachers give directions to places the students don't want to go. If you can't read well, there is no point in reading faster. The material must be good enough so that you won't throw it away afterward. We are trying to build attitudes in reading that will develop what Eric Hoffer calls "a terrific hunger for the printed word."

Today's parents and teachers are greatly concerned about the quality of *reading*. This, in turn, leads us to the quality of *writing*. Quotable, well-expressed ideas are often a stimulus for further reading and a source of inspiration and delight. Therefore, I hope this collection of thoughts will be a useful educational tool for recalling not only what was said but what was *well* said.

Edgar Dale
May 1983

Publisher's note: The reader will note that some of the quotes in this collection do not carry a source. Professor Dale's files of quotes collected over his lifetime did not carry a source for these items, but he graciously acknowledges the contributions of the authors, even if they must remain anonymous.

Action

Those who act receive the prizes.
— Aristotle

Wait and see vs. do and see.

I see and approve better things, but follow worse.
— Ovid

China will not change because of little things. A great revolution must come first.
— Chinese student

Adolescence

Adolescence is when you worry not only how your children will turn out but when they will turn in.

Prelude to disaster: "We have done everything for that boy."

Aging

On reaching 50: Think of it this way; you're a day closer to Social Security.

On being over 65: When I looked in the glass I was stunned with admiration; and it seemed to me that if I could have a grandfather like that I could die happy.

Middle-age is the time when you will do anything to feel better except to give up what's hurting you.

If you ask how I know that my youth is spent,
My get-up-and-go has got-up-and-went.
But sometimes I grin
When I think where it's been.

Growing old is when the gleam in your eye is the sun hitting your bifocals.

My hope is to have everybody die young as late as possible.
— Jean Mayer, nutritionist

He never found the time to grow old.

He had reached the age of statutory senility.

We should cease fighting age as if it were a foe . . . memories of past experiences may be even sweeter than these experiences were in reality.
— Ralph Sockman

Appreciation

Much of life is made of memories, warm and happy memories of small kindnesses and consideration, of courtesy, of constancy, consistency, a mother's attentive care, a father's kindliness, a child's thankfulness; thoughtfulness each day, not grand and rare and obvious outward acts — not all at once, but small and constant ways as each occasion comes. If we want happiness with loved ones, and peace, and quiet conscience, we need to learn the little lessons, the small services, the continuing kindnesses, the habitual acts of honesty, the constancy of cleanliness — not just one big washing. We don't stumble over mountains. We stumble over small things mostly.

— Richard L. Evans

The best portion of a good man's life,
His little nameless, unremembered acts
Of kindness and of love.

— William Wordsworth

It is one of the most beautiful compensations of this life, that no man can sincerely help another without helping himself.

— Samuel Smiles

Apathy, inertia, and self-consciousness prevent many from saying the gracious word of encouragement in those areas of human living where it is often so richly deserved. Unfortunately, adverse criticism seems much easier to offer than is commendation.

— Edgar Dale

I can live for two months on a good compliment.
—Mark Twain

A young woman, desperately ill and realizing perhaps that she did not have long to live, began thinking of some of her rich experiences as a student at a state university. She wrote a "thank-you" letter to the director of the university chorus. In his reply he said, "I have directed thousands of persons in choirs, and this is one of the very few notes of appreciation I have ever received."
—Edgar Dale

The other day I walked into the office of a jeweler who had done a good deal of work for me. I told him that the watch I had bought from him was working fine. The jeweler beamed and said, "You know, you are the first person in my whole life who ever came in and told me that his watch was running fine. The only people who talk to me are those who tell me their watches are out of order. I get all of the bad news about watches and none of the good."
—Edgar Dale

I was talking to a noted agricultural specialist who has saved farmers in one state at least a million dollars through his research and active work in the field. I asked, "How many letters have you received from farmers thanking you for these services?" He said, dryly, "I cannot remember one."
—Edgar Dale

If you have time to accept hospitality, you have time to write a thank-you note.

Flowers leave some of their fragrance in the hand that bestows them.
—Chinese proverb

Don't be a stingy receiver.
—Edgar Dale

Just praise is a debt and should be paid.
—old New England saying

Books

Books must be read as deliberately and reservedly as they were written.
> —Henry David Thoreau

We need not burn books to kill our civilization; we need only leave them unread for a generation.
> —Robert M. Hutchins

The multitude of books is a great evil. There is no measure or limit to this fever for writing; everyone must be an author; some out of vanity to acquire celebrity and raise up a name, others for the sake of lucre and gain.
> —Martin Luther

What harm can a book do that costs a hundred crowns? Twenty volumes folio will never cause a revolution; it is the little portable volumes of thirty sous that are to be feared.
> —Voltaire

What variety, what refreshment, and what interest would be found in books if authors wrote only what they thought!
> —Vauvenargues

Each age must write its own books; or rather, each generation for the next succeeding. The books of an older period will not fit this.
> —Ralph Waldo Emerson

I love such books as are either easy and entertaining, and that tickle my fancy, or such as give me comfort, and offer counsel in recording my life and death.

—Montaigne

People seldom read a book which is given to them. The way to spread a work is to sell it at a low price.

—Samuel Johnson

This man was a very sensible man, who perfectly understood common affairs; a man of a great deal of knowledge of the world, fresh from life, not strained through books.

—Samuel Johnson

In a way, the main fault of all books is that they are too long.

—Vauvenargues

I am always for getting a boy forward in his learning; for that is a sure good. I would let him at first read *any* English book which happens to engage his attention; because you have done a great deal, when you have brought him to have entertainment from a book. He'll get better books afterwards.

—Samuel Johnson

We live too much in books and not enough in nature, and we are very much like that simpleton of a Pliny the Younger, who went on studying a Greek author while before his eyes Vesuvius was overwhelming five cities beneath the ashes.

—Anatole France

I would never read a book if it were possible for me to talk half an hour with the man who wrote it.

—Woodrow Wilson

If one cannot enjoy reading a book over and over again, there is no use in reading it at all.

—Oscar Wilde

I cannot imagine a pleasanter old age than one spent in the not too remote country where I would reread and annotate my favorite books.

—André Maurois

Some books are to be tasted, others to be swallowed, and some few to be chewed and digested.
— Francis Bacon

There is no such thing as a moral or an immoral book. Books are well written, or badly written. That is all.
— Oscar Wilde

Life being very short, and the quiet hours of it few, we ought to waste none of them in reading valueless books.
— John Ruskin

When I am dead, I hope it may be said: "His sins were scarlet, but his books were read."
— Hillaire Belloc

Read no history, only biography, for that is life without theory.
— Benjamin Disraeli

Censors

Blessed are the censors for they shall inhibit the earth.
—Official Bulletin of England's
Guild of Film Critics

When a library expels a book of mine and leaves an unexpurgated Bible lying around where unprotected youth can get ahold of it, the deep unconscious irony of it delights me.
—Mark Twain

If all mankind minus one were of one opinion, and only one person were of the contrary opinion, mankind would be no more justified in silencing that one person, than he, if he had the power, would be justified in silencing mankind.
—John Stuart Mill

Be not intimidated, therefore, by any terrors, from publishing with the utmost freedom, whatever can be warranted by the laws of your country; nor suffer yourselves to be wheedled out of your liberty by any pretences of politeness, delicacy, or decency. These, as they are often used, are but three different names for hypocrisy, chicanery, and cowardice.
—John Adams, 1765

I see with indignation that the censorship of the press is to be established again, and the liberty of the press abolished. . . . It is of his conscience that the man of letters is now being robbed, of his artist's conscience.
—Gustave Flaubert at the age of
thirteen

Change

People don't resist change as much as the way they are changed.

One can cajole, ridicule, warn and still we shall remain lukewarm. It is easier for us to erect monuments and rename expressways and light eternal flames than it is for us to change.

—Stephen Rose

The greatest discovery of my generation is that human beings can alter their lives by altering their attitudes of mind.

—William James

The world changes faster than the people in it.

Nothing should be done for the first time, says the fearful man or woman.

We know our lakes are dying, our rivers growing filthier daily, our atmosphere increasingly polluted. We are aware of racial tensions that could tear the nation apart. We understand that oppressive poverty in the midst of affluence is intolerable. We see our cities sliding toward disaster. Yet we are seized by a kind of paralysis of the will. It's like a waking nightmare.

—John Gardner

The more things change, the more they are the same.

—Alphonse Karr

To grow is to change, and to become perfect is to have changed many times.

—Cardinal Newman

Nothing is more curious than the self-satisfied dogmatism with which mankind at each period of its history cherishes the delusion of finality of its existing modes of knowledge.

—Alfred North Whitehead

One of the things that you learn from history is that every generation of men is always going through a period of painful, critical, and destructive transition.

—Frank Underhill

Beware of all enterprises that require new clothes, and not rather a new wearer of clothes.

—Henry David Thoreau

Novelty is no substitute for quality.

We must be fearful of innovation without change.

Taking a new step, uttering a new word is what people fear most.

—Fyodor Dostoyevsky

Childhood

Hold childhood in reverence and do not be in any hurry to judge it for good or ill. Give nature time to work before you take over her tasks, lest you interfere with her method.
— Jean Jacques Rousseau

A difficult child is nearly always made difficult by wrong treatment at home. . . . The difficult child is the child who is unhappy. He is at war with himself; and in consequence, he is at war with the world.
— A. S. Neill

It is very difficult to cheat a gifted child out of making good use of his intellectual abilities, but it is very easy to cheat him of his childhood. . . . Enjoying childhood experiences to the full is the best preparation for becoming a mature adult.
— Bruno Bettelheim

A child's mind is like a bank — whatever you put in, you get back in ten years, with interest.
— Frederic Wertham

Choice

Though we sometimes speak of a primrose path we all know that a bad life is just as difficult, just as full of obstacles and hardships, as the good one. . . . The only choice is in the kind of life one would care to spend one's efforts on.

— John Erskine

If we are ever in doubt what to do, it is a good rule to ask ourselves what we shall wish on the morrow that we had done.

— Lord Avebury, John Lubbock

The law of consequences has not been repealed.

The power of choice is the power to keep options open.

Education in the humanities sharpens the individual's quality of choice. And in a free society, the choice is absolutely essential. Choice is a vital part of all our lives. And nowhere is it more important than in free government or a government of a free society.

In order to be in charge of our life we must be aware of both the little choices and the big choices we are making. We talk a lot about the big, dramatic choices we make in our lives. However, the daily little choices influence and indeed determine the big choices. Every day, wittingly or unwittingly, we choose whether we want to be more or less humane, more or less human.

— Edgar Dale

We *are* our choices.

— Jean-Paul Sartre

Asked by the psychologist whether she was indecisive, the patient replied: "Yes . . . and No."

Committees

A committee saves minutes and wastes hours.

A committee is a group of the unfit, appointed by the unwilling, to do the unnecessary.

Never has so little been done by so many.

They are so busy cooperating that no one is doing any work.

Graffiti: Where is the modern university headed? To a committee meeting.

A committee is a group that does together what's tough or even impossible to do alone.

A committee is a group that has a commitment.

To get the job done, a committee should consist of three persons, two of whom are absent.

Faculty meeting: I came, I saw, I concurred.

The purpose of a meeting is to assemble people who aren't doing anything, to talk about doing something, and hence feel that they have accomplished something. It aims to accomplish by talk what has not been accomplished by action.

If the members of some committees were laid end to end, it would help.

A committee is a group of people who can claim lack of responsibility if their work fails and credit for it if it succeeds.

Communication

Knowledge that is not communicated has a way of turning the mind sour.
> —C. Wright Mills

There is no worse lie than a truth misunderstood by those who hear it.
> —William James

There is one thing worse than not communicating: it is thinking you have communicated when you have not.
> —Edgar Dale

If we maximize communication, we can minimize coercion.
> —Edgar Dale

Communication doesn't flow. Sometimes it leaks, spurts, and dribbles.
> —Edgar Dale

You can be an expert in your subject but not be expert in communicating that subject.
> —Edgar Dale

He had nothing to say, and fortunately said it incomprehensibly.

Communication is a process of sharing experience till it becomes a common possession. It modifies the disposition of both parties who partake in it.
> —John Dewey

What corrupts communication? Anger, fear, prejudice, egotism, and envy.

To communicate well you must know your subject and also how much of it you plan to communicate to your students.

On certain days they did not exchange a word. On other days they chatted. They understood each other to perfection without saying a word, because they liked the same things and had similar feelings.

—Guy de Maupassant

A gossip is one who talks to you about others; a bore is one who talks to you about himself; a brilliant conversationalist is one who talks to you about yourself.

Unless your tongue utters language that is readily understood, how can people make out what you say? You will be pouring words into empty air! There are ever so many kinds of language in the world, every one of them meaning something. Well, unless I understand the meaning of what is said to me, I shall appear to the speaker to be talking gibberish, and to my mind he will be talking gibberish himself.

—I Corinthians 12: 9-11
Moffatt Edition

An honest tale speeds best being plainly told.

—William Shakespeare

He only believes what he overhears.

Your ideas cannot become my ideas just because I read them. They become mine when I test them by acting on them.

Since we have two ears and one mouth, we should listen twice as much as we talk.

It is better to talk it out in a forum than to fight it out in an arena.

If you can't communicate, the least you can do is to shut up.

—Tom Lehrer

In language clarity is everything.
—Confucius

To hear is to forget, to see is to know, to do is to understand.

While your head is in the lion's mouth, stroke his back.
—African proverb

A president of a large corporation wrote a letter to his ten vice-presidents suggesting that their letters and memoranda were often too long. The next morning he had on his desk nine letters bearing only the single word: "Right!" The tenth letter merely said: "Check!"
—Edgar Dale

Good communication is personal.
—Edgar Dale

The definition of communication that I like best is called archaic by the dictionary. It describes communication as meaning "to share in common, to participate in."
—Edgar Dale

An omnipresent barrier to communication lies in the fact that people who live differently think differently.
—Edgar Dale

The chief problem of this generation and succeeding generations is to put people in touch with each other — in mind and heart.
—Edgar Dale

We have still to insure . . . that all that can be thought and known is kept plainly, honestly, and easily available to the ordinary men and women who are the substance of mankind.
—H. G. Wells

It takes your enemy and your friend, working together, to hurt you to the heart; the one to slander you and the other to get the news to you.
—Mark Twain

It takes two to communicate.
—Edgar Dale

There is a time to say something,
There is a time to say nothing,
But there is no time to say everything.

Every communication a manager makes does two things: it conveys ideas and it generates feelings. The reader's feelings, needs and motives must be considered as well as his literacy level.
—Royal Bank of Canada
Monthly Letter, January 1971

Every communication must comply with certain essential requirements and these are sincerity, honesty, and truthfulness. Good intentions and a clear conscience do not thereby make a communication sound and reliable. A communication must state the truth. It must accurately reflect the situation with all its implications. The moral worth and validity of any communication do not lie solely in its theme or intellectual content. The way in which it is presented, the way in which it is spoken and treated and even the audience for which it is designed — all these factors must be taken into account.
—Pope Paul VI

Not that the story need be long, but it will take a long while to make it short.
—Henry David Thoreau

On the basis of available research the effectiveness of a particular instructional material is more dependent upon the nature and quality of the message than upon the characteristics of the channel of communication.
—*Encyclopedia of Educational Research*, 4th ed. 1969

It isn't the medium that's at fault, it's the tedium of the medium.
—Edgar Dale

A pedant is a man who says what everybody knows in language that no one understands.

A writer thinks with his fingers. A speaker thinks with his tongue.

A captive audience is rarely captivated.

No one wants to take bad news to the king.

Many argue; not many converse.
　　　　　　　　　　　　　—Louisa May Alcott

Let thy speech be short, comprehending much in few words.
　　　　　　　　　　　　　—Ecclesiasticus 32:17

The more you say, the less people remember. The fewer the words, the greater the profit.
　　　　　　　　　　　　　—Fenelon

The wisdom of nations lies in their proverbs, which are brief and pithy.
　　　　　　　　　　　　　—William Penn

Every speaker is his own most interested and affected listener.
　　　　　　　　　　　　　—Wendell Johnson

A commencement speech is supposed to be brief to satisfy the students, profound to satisfy the faculty, and dramatic to satisfy the press.

Society is held together by communication and information.
　　　　　　　　　　　　　—James Boswell

All caring has hazards; the outcomes are uncertain. To care for others and to let them care for us is a creative experiment in communication in which we may get hurt. But the price paid, the risk of being wounded, is the price of all communication. It is because we ourselves are hurt that we can understand the hurts of others. The sensitive heart is not cheaply bought.
　　　　　　　　　　　　　—Edgar Dale

Creativity

In today's world creativity is not just a nice thing to have. It is a grave necessity. We need more innovation and invention, first, to save the world from self-destruction, and second, to contribute to the mental health and power of individuals. Imitating the past is not good enough; only the creative society will survive.

—Edgar Dale

A university is a professor on one end of a dialogue and a questioning student at the other.

The imitative student if given a question will answer it. The creative student if given an answer will question it.

—Edgar Dale

There is nothing more difficult to take in hand, more perilous to conduct, or more uncertain in its success than to take the lead in the introduction of a new order of things.

—Niccolo Machiavelli

Human nature has a much greater genius for sameness than for originality.

—James Russell Lowell

That we have untapped potential for creativity is shown by the fact that most of us while asleep produce dreams far beyond our ordinary capacity for subtlety and range.

—Gardner Murphy

To give a fair chance to potential creativity is a matter of life and death for any society. This is all-important, because the outstanding creative ability of a fairly small percentage of the population is mankind's ultimate capital asset, and the only one with which only man has been endowed.

— Arnold Toynbee

Democracy

Democracy is the only system of government that trusts in its own persuasiveness, so that all the winds of doctrine have way within it. Democracy is the only system that has faith in the free mind. Democracy is the only system that does not make education the servant of power.

— R. M. MacIver

Though the will of the majority is in all cases to prevail, that will, to be rightful, must be reasonable. The minority possess their equal rights which equal laws must protect and to violate would be oppression.

— Thomas Jefferson

In a democracy no man has the right to be ignorant about the basic institutions under which he lives. He may have other rights but he does not have this one.

— Edgar Dale

For a majority rule to be democratic it must offer the minority a chance to become a majority. If it does not, the so-called cultural democracy of the majority can become a tyranny, an enemy of democracy.

— Edgar Dale

Discipline

We must learn to stick to something we're not stuck on.
— Edgar Dale

The memory strengthens as you lay burdens upon it.
— Thomas De Quincey

Permissiveness is for disciplined people.

The longest road in the world is the one between aspiration and achievement.

There never has been, and cannot be, a good life without self-control.
— Leo Tolstoy

It is a calumny upon men to say that they are aroused to heroic action by ease, hope of pleasure, sugar plums of any kind, in this world or the next.
— Thomas Carlyle

. . . the final performance, which may take a minute, has been preceded by many hours of rehearsal.
— Logan Pearsal Smith

It is easier to suppress the first desire than to satisfy all that follow it.
— Benjamin Franklin

Education

That's what education means, to be able to do what you've never done before.
—Alice Freeman Palmer

Everything educates, and some things educate more than others.
—Harold Taylor

Education: That which discloses to the wise and disguises from the foolish their lack of understanding.
—Ambrose Bierce

The problem of education is to help the pupil see the forest by means of the trees.
—Edgar Dale

As things are now, education is so cluttered and tangled up with a thousand senseless notions and stupidities, that the task of reformation is almost a superhuman one. It is entirely a task of taking away and reducing — not one of adding to, or explaining. It is the task of the sculptor, who cuts the superfluous marble off, rather than that of the wax-workman, who lays on the stuff thicker and thicker . . .
—Walt Whitman

You do not get an education in college. You learn *how* to get an education and to develop a taste for it.

Some students are so busy going to classes they have little time to get an education.
— Edgar Dale

You may not divide the seamless cloak of learning. There is only one subject-matter for education and that is Life in all its manifestations.
— Alfred North Whitehead

Education is the disciplined connection of the unconnected.

We need higher education, not further education. Higher education means more responsibility for one's own education.

Education replaces cocksure ignorance with thoughtful uncertainty.
— *Miles of Smiles*

Education is a problem of getting our bearings, of developing orientation, of discovering in what direction to go and how to get there.
— Edgar Dale

It a man empties his purse into his head, no one can take it from him.
— Benjamin Franklin

My definition of an educated man is the fellow who knows the right thing to do at the time it has to be done.
— Charles Kettering

The university, without abandoning its admirable relation to the state, must be the capital and fortress of thought. Emerson's definition of the scholar still holds: it is man thinking. This is the core of the university idea, and if we lose it, we lose everything. Can we somehow at once combine and separate the two aspects of American university life — the day-to-day serviceability to the state that public universities so admirably have developed, and the protection of man thinking in the light of time and eternity? To protect that man is the quintessential service of the university to the state.
— Howard Mumford Jones

Education aims to expand, amplify, deepen and to refine the quality and continuity of one's experiences, to extend each person's radius of concern.
—Edgar Dale

Five hundred years of education for freedom would make intelligent human beings of us and it wouldn't matter any more what color we were. But we have run out of time.
—Milton Mayer

Education involves that part of a task which moves beyond the routine, the particular, the predictable and into the novel, the general, the unpredictable. Education is serendipitous, returns compound interest on our investment of time and energy.
—Edgar Dale

A professor asked a mature woman who had just enrolled at Ohio State University: "What do you intend to use your education for?" "For my increased enjoyment," she replied.

'Tis education forms the common mind;
Just as the twig is bent the tree's inclined.
—Alexander Pope

The best claim that a college education can possibly make on your respect, the best thing it can aspire to accomplish for you, is this: that it should help you to know a good man when you see him.
—William James

Excellence

The quest for the best

The excellent becomes the permanent.
— Jane Addams

We have an overabundance of mediocrity and a shortage of excellence.

The aim of an education is to put each child in touch with the best.

The autocatalytic effect of a good faculty . . . if you have good ones, you can get more good ones.
— George W. Beadle

A technological society can produce an abundance of everything except excellence.

If you did your best yesterday, you've begun to die; if you're doing your best today, you're beginning to live!
— *Northwest Sparkler*

The best way to make a person critical is to show him the first-rate till anything inferior ceases to attract.
— Sir Richard Livingston

A great society not only searches out excellence but rewards it when it is found.

What the best and wisest parent wants for his own child, that must the community want for all of its children.

— John Dewey

There is danger in probing the future with too short a stick. Excellence takes time.

— Edgar Dale

Experience

The best substitute for experience is being 16.
— *The Branson* (Missouri)
White River Leader

Personal experience is all the experience we ever have.

I have but one lamp by which my feet are guided, and that is the lamp of experience. I know of no way of judging of the future but by the past.
— Patrick Henry

Don't keep forever on the public road, going only where others have gone. Leave the beaten track occasionally and drive into the woods. You will be certain to find something you have never seen before. Of course it will be a little thing, but do not ignore it. Follow it up, explore all around it; one discovery will lead to another, and before you know it you will have something worth thinking about to occupy your mind. All really big discoveries are the results of thought.
— Alexander Graham Bell

Experience alone cannot deliver to us necessary truths; truths completely demonstrated by reason. Its conclusions are particular, not universal.
— John Dewey

Experience is not what happens to a man. It is what a man does with what happens to him.
— Aldous Huxley

The best substitute for experience is going to college.

Experience is the child of thought, and thought is the child of action. We cannot learn men from books.
—Benjamin Disraeli

We should be careful to get out of an experience only the wisdom that is in it — and stop there; lest we be like the cat that sits down on a hot stove-lid. She will never sit down on a hot stove-lid again — and that is well; but also she will never sit down on a cold one anymore.
—Mark Twain

Freedom

Many politicians of our time are in the habit of laying it down, as a self-evident proposition, that no people ought to be free till they are fit to use their freedom. The maxim is worthy of the fool in the old story, who resolved not to go into the water till he had learned to swim. If men are to wait for liberty till they become wise and good in slavery, they may indeed wait forever.

—Thomas Babington Macaulay

Use freedom or it atrophies.

In 1853 Karl Marx asked, Will the great Russian state ever halt its march toward world power? He answered, Russia has only one opponent: the explosive power of democratic ideas and the unborn urge of the human race in the direction of human freedom.

We are not so absurd as to propose that the teacher should not set forth his own opinions as the true ones, and exert his utmost powers to exhibit their truth in the strongest light. To abstain from this would be to nourish the worst intellectual habit of all, that of not finding, and not looking for, certainty in anything. But the teacher himself should not be held to any creed; nor should the question be, whether his own opinions are the true ones, but whether he is well instructed in those of other people, and, in enforcing his own, states the arguments for all conflicting opinions fairly.

—John Stuart Mill

There are two freedoms: the false where a man is free to do what he likes; the true where a man is free to do what he ought.
— Charles Kingsley

The only freedom which deserves the name is that of pursuing our own good in our own way, so long as we do not attempt to deprive others of theirs, or impede their efforts to obtain it.
— John Stuart Mill

I shall begin to believe that we care more for freedom than we do for imposing our own beliefs upon others in order to subject them to our will, when I see that the main purpose of our schools and other institutions is to develop powers of unremitting and discriminating observation and judgment.
— John Dewey

The liberty of the individual must be thus far limited; that he must not make a nuisance of himself to other people.
— John Stuart Mill

Future

What is the use of living, if it be not to strive for noble causes and to make this muddled world a better place for those who will live in it after we are gone? How else can we put ourselves in harmonious relation with the great verities and consolations of the infinite and the external? I avow my faith that we are marching towards better days. Humanity will not be cast down. We are going on — swinging bravely forward along the grand high road — and already behind the distant mountains is the promise of the sun.

— Winston Churchill

It's better to go down pushing forward than it is to walk backwards into the future.

— Edgar Dale

The greatest liberation of thought achieved by the scientific revolution was to have given human beings a sense of a future in this world.

— P. B. Medawar

The fact that we don't have *all* the answers does not mean that we have none. We know enough things for sure to produce huge surpluses of wheat, and send nearly all children to school. We don't know for sure what we should teach and how to teach it.

The good old days are now.

— Milton Caniff

The dogmas of the quiet past are inadequate to the stormy present . . . As our case is new, so we must think anew and act anew.

— Abraham Lincoln

We should all be concerned about the future because that is where we will spend the remainder of our lives.

— Charles F. Kettering

. . . Come, my friends, 'Tis not too late to seek a newer world.

— Alfred Lord Tennyson

Human resources and natural resources are inexorably inter-twined, and tomorrow's children, if they are to manage this land well, will need the precision of scientifically attuned minds, coupled with a sensitivity to their fellow men (and fellow women) and creatures.

— John F. Kennedy

It is easy to be in tune with the past; it is tough to be in tune with the future.

Human Relations

The worst sin toward our fellow creatures is not to hate them, but to be indifferent to them.

—George Bernard Shaw

We have met the enemy, and he is us.

—Pogo

An osteopath is a person who rubs you the right way.

If you treat an individual as he is, he will stay as he is, but if you treat him as if he were what he ought to be and could be, he will become what he ought to be and what he could be.

—Goethe

O world, I cannot hold thee close enough!

—Edna St. Vincent Millay

Everyone is a moon, and has a dark side which he never shows to anybody.

—Mark Twain

Christ leads us to put ourselves out in order to take friends in. He inspired us to see good in persons we never noticed or liked.

—Ralph W. Sockman

To the person who says, "I know what I like," we can only reply, "You like what you know."

—Edgar Dale

Evidently he had taken a lot of courses in insensitivity training.
— Edgar Dale

People must never be humiliated — that is the main thing.
— Anton Chekov

People develop feelings that they are liked, wanted, acceptable, and able from having been liked, wanted, accepted, and from having been successful. One learns that he is these things, not from being told but only through the experience of being treated as though he were so. Here is the key to what must be done to produce more adequate people.
— Arthur W. Coombs

A father gave his son a copy of *How to Win Friends and Influence People*. Son returned it to his father the next day with the simple comment: "Too mechanical."

Ideas

On the clarity of your ideas depends the scope of your success in any endeavor.

> —Horace Greeley

An idea is information with legs on it.

> —Edgar Dale

Half-baked ideas are all right as long as they are in the oven.

> —Edgar Dale

Ignorance

Ignorance is a poor tool in a battle of wits.

If ignorance is bliss, why aren't more people happy?

No nation is permitted to live in ignorance with impunity.
                                    —Thomas Jefferson

Imagination

Imagination is more important than knowledge. Knowledge is limited, whereas imagination embraces the entire world — stimulating progress, giving birth to evolution.

—Albert Einstein

The virtue of imagination is its reaching, by intuition and intensity, a more essential truth than is seen at the surface of things.

—John Ruskin

Only the poet can look beyond the detail and see the whole picture.

—Helen Hayes

Individualism

I desire that there be as many different persons in the world as possible; I would have each one be very careful to find out and pursue his own way.

—Henry David Thoreau

Everyone carries within himself a productive uniqueness as the nucleus of his being.

—Nietzsche

Underneath all, I swear nothing is good to me now that ignores individuals.

—Walt Whitman

Individual means "not divided."

To be nobody-but-myself — in a world which is doing its best, night and day, to make you everybody else — means to fight the hardest battle which any human being can fight, and never stop fighting.

—E. E. Cummings

You cannot put the same shoe on every foot.

—Publius Syrus

If a man does not keep pace with his companions, perhaps it is because he hears a different drummer. Let him step to the music which he hears, however measured or far away.

—Henry David Thoreau

While to the claims of charity a man may yield and yet be free, to the claims of conformity no man may yield and be free at all.

— Oscar Wilde

Not armies, not nations have advanced the race; but here and there, in the course of ages, an individual has stood up and cast his shadow over the world.

— E. H. Chapin

Every man is an exception.

— Sören Kierkegaard

Innovation

He that will not apply new remedies must expect new evils for time is the greatest innovator.
—Francis Bacon

We don't change fast because the model presented by the reformer seems not worth the trouble.

The sequence in the acceptance of a new idea:
1. It's a foolish idea and won't work.
2. It's not a bad idea, but the time isn't ripe.
3. The time is ripe, but we couldn't finance it.
4. I was always in favor of this idea.
   —Edgar Dale

Be not the first by whom the new is tried,
Nor yet the last to lay the old aside.
—Alexander Pope

Intelligence

Intelligentsia — people educated beyond their intelligence.

The average man thinks his intelligence is above average.

Intelligence is what the other fellow lacks.

Though there is no substitute for intelligence, it is not enough. There are human beings who have intelligence but do not have the moral courage to act on it. On the other hand, moral courage without intelligence is dangerous. It leads to fanaticism. Education should develop both intelligence *and* courage.

— Sidney Hook

Inventions

How did we ever get along without scotch tape?

The wheel was man's greatest invention until he got behind it.

The fellow who invented the wheel wasn't the real hero — how about the guy who came up with the idea of the other three?

Knowledge

Knowledge is the property of him who can use it. Knowledge creates interest. With skillful teaching, your students will show more and more interest with increasing knowledge of the subject. Never forget the motivational effects of knowledge.

— Joseph Kennedy

Knowledge is increasing faster than we can distribute it. We increase knowledge at electronic speed, distribute it with a horse and buggy.

— Edgar Dale

If a little knowledge is dangerous, where is the man who has so much as to be out of danger?

— Thomas Henry Huxley

That knowledge is of most worth which enables us to get or generate more knowledge and to test it to make sure it is knowledge.

— Edgar Dale

Scholar — one who tries to find his own mistakes.

Knowledge begets knowledge. There is always a need to know more.

Teach thy tongue to say, "I don't know."

— Talmud

Knowledge is of two kinds: we know a subject ourselves, or we know where we can find information upon it.
— James Boswell

Information isn't knowledge till you can use it.

Knowledge changes knowledge.

You need to know what you don't need to know.

Language

We have really everything in common with America nowadays, except, of course, language.
— George Bernard Shaw

The difficulty of learning foreign languages is suggested in different countries by the fact that even animals speak different languages. American dogs say "bow wow" when they bark; the French dog says "gnaf, gnaf"; the Japanese "wan, wan"; the Norwegian dog "vov, vov."

Foreign language instruction helps many high school students become illiterate in two languages.
— Edgar Dale

Few high school students look upon the language which they speak and write as an art, not merely as a tool. Yet it is, or ought to be, the noblest of all the arts, looked upon with respect, even with reverence, and used always with care, courtesy, and the deepest respect.
— Mary Ellen Chase

The cat chased the mouse into its hole and waited beside the hole. Then it barked like a dog. The mouse, thinking the cat had gone away, came out of its hole and was pounced on. Then the cat said archly, "You see, it pays to be bilingual."

Language is by all odds the most subtle and powerful technique we have for controlling other people.
— George A. Miller

To learn a second language you must murder it.
　　　　　　　　　　　　—Otto Jespersen

Language is not only the vehicle of thought; it is also the driver.
　　　　　　　　　　　　—Ludwig Wittgenstein

Language is not an abstract construction of the learned, or of dictionary-makers, but is something arising out of the work, needs, ties, joys, affections, tastes, of long generations of humanity, and has its bases broad and low, close to the ground.
　　　　　　　　　　　　—Walt Whitman

The only difference between man and beasts is Syntax.
　　　　　　　　　　　　—Herbert Read

Learning

We worship the quantity of practice and ignore the quality.

Learning is a treasure which follows its owner everywhere.
— Chinese proverb

There is not one course of study which merely gives general culture and another which gives special knowledge. . . . You may not divide the seamless cloak of learning.
— Alfred North Whitehead

Punishment is the absence of reward.

"What did I do that was right?" asked the beginning golfer who made a hole in one.

In the classroom there is more teaching than learning. Outside the classroom there is more learning than teaching.

Listening

You don't need a research study to prove there is more talking than there is listening.

A wise man will hear and will increase learning.
— Proverbs 1:5

If you ask: "Why don't *we* listen?" the reply is that *the speakers* aren't interesting. If you ask, "Why don't *they* listen?" the reply is: "*They* are not interested." We tend to put the burden of interest on the other fellow.
— Edgar Dale

What a mercy it would be if we were able to open and close our ears as easily as we open and close our eyes!
— G. C. Lichtenberg

Explanation given by a pupil for not joining in discussions: "I think I'll learn more by listening. Anything I would say I already know."

Know how to listen and you will profit even from those who talk badly.
— Plutarch

We learn to listen and we listen to learn.

I know that you believe you understand what you think I said, but I am not sure you realize that what you heard is not what I meant.

You have seen much but remembered little, your ears are wide open but nothing is heard.

—Isaiah 42:20

You earn the right to speak by listening.

The only way to entertain some folks is to listen to them.

—Kin Hubbard

It takes a great man to make a good listener.

—Sir Arthur Helps

The grace of listening is lost if the listener's attention is demanded, not as a favor, but as a right.

—Pliny the Younger

Nothing increases the respect and gratitude of one man for another more than when he is heard exactly and with interest.

—R. Umbach

Give us grace to listen well.

—John Keble

Love

Against the superiority of another the only remedy is love.
— Goethe

A child is not born loving or hateful. Love and hate are learned. We have to learn to use ourselves to teach young people to learn to love.
— Jack Frymier

To understand is not only to pardon but in the end to love.
— Walter Lippmann

Shall we make a new rule of life from tonight: always to be a little kinder than necessary?
— James M. Barrie

He drew a circle that shut me out —
Heretic, rebel, a thing to flout.
But Love and I had the wit to win:
We drew a circle that took him in.
— Edwin Markham

Faults are thick where love is thin.
— James Howell

To love, be lovable.
— Roman poet

One of our greatest learning tasks is how to give and receive love.

When the satisfaction or the security of another person becomes as significant to one as is one's own security, then the state of love exists.

—Harry Stack Sullivan

There is no fear in love; but perfect love casteth out fear; because fear hath torment. He that feareth is not made perfect in love.

—I John 4:18

Eve: Adam, do you love me?
Adam: Who else?

Are children grateful for what their parents do for them? They should be, considering how often they have heard about it. But caring and loving must not be evaluated too soon. Caring takes time. Love is patient.

—Edgar Dale

Money

Money goes where the money is.

Money isn't everything but it does help you keep in touch with your relatives.

Thrift is a wonderful virtue, especially in one's ancestors.

He was always a dollar short and an hour late.

If you think kids today don't know the value of money, try giving one a nickel.

A man said, "My only extravagance is that I like to spend money."

It's good to have money and the things that money can buy; but it's good to check up once in a while and make sure you haven't lost the things that money can't buy.
— Edgar Dale

Money isn't the most important thing in the world, but it is mighty close to what is first.

He always had too much month left at the end of the money.

He spent his money and his money spent him.

Will: "Being of sound mind, I spent every cent when I was alive."

By the time you have money to burn, the fire has gone out.

The persons most concerned with keeping up with the Joneses are their creditors.

A budget is where you worry twice about what you spend.

The world consists of three groups: the haves, the have-nots, and those with credit cards.
> —Edgar Dale

No man but a blockhead ever wrote except for money.
> —James Boswell

When a dollar was worth a dollar I didn't have a dime.
> —New York taxi driver

Why do you rob banks?
That's where the money is.
> —Willy Sutton

Money is the seed of money.
> —Jean Jacques Rousseau

Never ask of money spent
Where the spender thinks it went.
Nobody was ever meant
To remember or invent.

It wasn't the principle he worried about; it was the money.

A husband walked into the house completely out of breath. "What happened, Honey?" asked his concerned wife. "It's a great new idea I have," he gasped. "I ran home all the way behind the bus and saved 50 cents." "Well, that certainly wasn't very bright," answered his wife. "Why didn't you run home behind a taxi and save three dollars?"
> —*Rotempary*, Tempe, Arizona

It's difficult to save money when your neighbors keep buying things you can't afford.

Remember this, if you are ever going to play professional sports. It is just that. A profession. A big time business and a player is only a hunk of meat on the block and good for only so long before spoilage sets in.

—Bill Russell

The best brains still tend to serve wealth, not people; the greatest rewards go to money-making, not public service. Our vocabulary tells our scale of values: a brewery, we say, is "free enterprise" while TVA is "socialism"; an AT&T bond issue is an "investment" while a government issue for social welfare is a "deficit"; the manufacturer of thalidomide pills is a "business executive"; the little gray-haired woman in HEW who saves the infants is a "bureaucrat."

—Louis J. Halle

Observing

Sherlock Holmes to Dr. Watson: "You *see* but you do not observe."

No matter where you are, watch people. . . Watch how they walk, how they move, how they turn around. Too many of us walk through life with blinders on our eyes. We see only what concerns us, instead of what goes on around us. . . I am trying to make you *see*!

—Advice from director D.W.
Griffith to actress Lillian Gish

With what words, oh writer, can you with a like perfection describe the whole arrangement of that of which the design is here? . . . I counsel you not to cumber yourself with words unless you are speaking to the blind. If, however notwithstanding, you wish to demonstrate to the ears rather than to the eyes of men, let your speech be of things of substance and natural things, and do not busy yourself in making enter by the ears things which have to do with the eyes, for in this you will be far surpassed by the work of the painter.

—Leonardo da Vinci

Perception is selective: A bald person sees non-bald men as abnormally hairy.

We can only see in a picture what our experience permits us to see.

—Edgar Dale

At a station in a dry valley of the interior, when I asked one of the resident scientists the reason for a spectacular peculiarity in the formation of the glaciers all around us, he answered: "I don't know, I'm a meteorologist, not a glaciologist." I was left to wonder what kind of a meteorologist it was who remained so uninterested in phenomena that were, after all, the products of meteorological circumstances.

—Louis Halle

God hides things by putting them near us.

—Ralph Waldo Emerson

Try to observe what you see.

We cannot create observers by saying, "observe," but by giving them the power and the means for this observation, and these means are procured through education of the senses. Once we have *aroused* such activity, auto-education is assured, for refined well-trained senses lead us to a closer observation of the environment, and this, with its infinite variety, attracts the attention and continues the psychosensory education.

—Maria Montessori

To observations which ourselves we make,
We grow more partial for the observer's sake.

—Alexander Pope

The eye does not see what the mind is unwilling to look at.

The eye sees what the mind knows.

Parents

A boy doesn't want his father to be a pal, he wants him to be a father.

Few parents have the courage and independence to care more for their children's happiness than for their "success."
— Erich Fromm

Parents say that they are not good at the new mathematics. They weren't very good at the old math either.

When I was a boy of 14, my father was so ignorant I could hardly stand to have the old man around. But when I got to be 21, I was astonished at how much he had learned in seven years.
— Mark Twain

Approximately the same ideas are shared by my parents and me except on politics, religion and philosophies.
— Donald Pearce

Father's commenting on use of family car: "There used to be a big argument as to who would get the car. So I put my foot down and whenever I want the car I just take it."

Potential

Some measure of genius is the rightful inheritance of every man.

— Alfred North Whitehead

Everything that enlarges the sphere of human powers, that shows man he can do what he thought he could not do, is valuable.

— James Boswell

There is no such thing as genius. Some children are less damaged than others.

— R. Buckminster Fuller

Don't say, "I can't." Say "I choose not to."

Men show their superiority inside; animals, outside.

— Russian proverb

Everyone excels in something in which another fails.

— Publius Syrus

No one knows what he can do till he tries.

— Publius Syrus

Men do not care how nobly they live, but only how long; although it is within the reach of every man to live nobly, but within no man's power to live long.

— Seneca

Compared to what we ought to be we are only half awake. Our fires are dampened, our drafts are checked. We are making use of only a small part of our mental and physical resources.

— William James

Professors

A professor is a man who has a lot to say and tries to say it all at once.

Today's professors are no more absent-minded than before, but certainly they are more absent.

The professor has one eye on the clouds, the other on a footnote.

A professor condenses a 10-minute talk into a one-hour lecture.

A professor is a man who puts his best footnote forward.

A professor has so much to say about what he means he gets you all confused.

A professor is a man who talks in someone else's sleep.

A professor is not necessarily smarter than other people but he does have his ignorance better organized.

A sociology professor calls a strip-tease a progressive disclosure.

A professor talks by the yard and listens by the inch.

If you ask a professor for the time of day, he'll give you a detailed history of the clock.

A professor talks with commas and semi-colons, not periods.

A professor has mastered the art of making the simple complex.

A professor keeps answering questions that nobody asked.

A professor of education lectures against the lecture method.

A professor tells students that telling isn't teaching, and spends most of his time telling them.

Questions

Young Rabi . . . went to the public schools and stood at the top of his class with little effort. He remembers vividly how his mother would tirelessly inquire, "Did you ask any good questions in school today?"

—Frances Bellow

We are often searching for better answers when we should be developing better questions.

A question is a trap and an answer is your foot in it.

—John Steinbeck

Watch for the question behind the question. The child is trying to organize his world.

The way a question is asked limits and disposes the ways in which any answer to it — right or wrong — may be given.

—Susanne K. Langer

A wise question is half of knowledge.

—Lord Bacon

We must ask many of the significant questions before we start the research.

There cannot be a precise answer to a vague question.

—Samuel Johnson

One small girl remained on the bus. Gently, the driver asked, "Do you know where you get off, honey?" "Yes," replied the tot, nodding firmly. "Where I got on!"
—Edith Kelly

Schools do not usually teach the art of questioning, but expect students to develop skill in answering questions that teachers didn't ask.
—Edgar Dale

The educated man knows which question can be answered precisely and which probably cannot be.
—Edgar Dale

Every question does not deserve an answer.
—Publius Syrus

Schools spend too much time teaching answers and too little on teaching how to question answers.

There is no right answer to a wrong question.

Reading

If you believe everything, you'd better not read.
— Japanese proverb

If books are critically written, they deserve to be critically read.
— Edgar Dale

You cannot be well-read unless you read well.
— Edgar Dale

When I am reading a book, whether wise or silly, it seems to be alive and talking to me.
— Jonathan Swift

Dad, why do they have to say everything three times?
— boy using first-grade reader

One must be a wise reader to quote wisely and well.
— A. B. Alcott

Read, not to contradict and confute; not to believe and take for granted; not to find talk and discourse; but to weigh and consider.
— Francis Bacon

The sagacious reader who is capable of reading between these lines what does not stand written in them, but is nevertheless implied, will be able to form some conception.
— Goethe

The act of injuring one's own mind or health, is a vice; and therefore it is the duty of parents and instructors, to prevent youth, peremptorily, from contracting the alluring habit of reading novels; which besides destroying the health, by incessant night reading, fits the mind for a world of fiction and romance, instead of a world of realities. If youth could be prevailed on first to taste the salutary sweets of Biography, History, Travels, Morality, Natural Philosophy and Geography, they would ever after, with rare exception, view a Novel with as much disgust as the mother of beautiful living children would a *doll*.

—N. Jesse Torrey

Books serve as a screen to keep us from a knowledge of things.

—William Hazlitt

From the moment I picked your book up until I laid it down I was convulsed with laughter. Some day I intend reading it.

—Groucho Marx

In literature as in love, we are astonished at what is chosen by others.

—André Maurois

Reading maketh a full man, conference a ready man, and writing an exact man.

—Francis Bacon

The bookful blockhead, ignorantly read,
With loads of learned lumber in his head.

—Alexander Pope

What is read twice is commonly better remembered than what is transcribed.

—Samuel Johnson

You write with ease to show your breeding,
But easy writing's curst hard reading.

—Richard Brinsley Sheridan

Never read any book that is not a year old.

—Ralph Waldo Emerson

A man ought to read just as inclination leads him; for what he reads as a task will do him little good. A young man should read five hours in a day, and so may acquire a great deal of knowledge.

— James Boswell

I cannot see that lectures can do so much good as reading the books from which the lectures are taken.

— James Boswell

I can find my biography in every fable that I read.

— Ralph Waldo Emerson

You develop good taste by tasting good things.

Discrimination is good taste often exercised.

You can't fall in love with books without being emotional about it.

Not every student can or should be taught methods of increasing his reading speed. One who has difficulty understanding what he reads will not be helped by learning to misunderstand faster.

—Edgar Dale

Reading is seeing by proxy.

— Herbert Spencer

You read what you are and you are what you read.

— Edgar Dale

In science, read by preference the newest works; in literature, the oldest. The classics are always modern.

— Edward Bulwer-Lytton

Read, mark, learn, and inwardly digest.

— Collect for the second Sunday in Advent

He that I am reading seems always to have the most force.

— Montaigne

Reading is easy if you already know how to do it.
— Edgar Dale

And does anyone seriously believe that a half-hour dramatization on television of some historical event or some current problem actually can convey as much as could be learned in the same time by reading twenty or thirty pages of a well-written composition? The truth is that most of the "modern" methods of communication are inefficient, wasteful, and inadequate when addressed to anyone competent to read.
— Joseph Wood Krutch

The poor reader's difficulty is rarely a mechanical problem; it is usually an inadequacy in perceiving or associating meaning with word and other language symbols.
— Paul A. Witty

To note the key importance of reading is not to neglect the significance of first-hand experience or semi-concrete experiences in the new mass media. Life is a recurring cycle of concrete to abstract to concrete. The highest levels of abstract thinking are anchored to life by the everyday concrete experiences of birth, life, and death. The symbol and its meaning are inextricably interwoven. All media contribute to the ability to use symbols effectively throughout life.
— Edgar Dale

Reading, we must remember, is a process of getting meaning from the printed page by putting meaning into the printed page. Reading taste and ability are always tethered to past experience. But reading itself is one way of increasing this capital fund of past experience. Reading, therefore, must be seen as more than *saying* the word, more than *seeing* the sentences and paragraphs. Good reading is the way a person brings his whole life to bear on the new ideas which he finds on the printed page. It is reading the lines, reading between the lines, and reading beyond the lines. It is an active, not a passive, process. The good reader becomes involved with the writing and the writer. He agrees, he argues back. He asks: Is it true? Is it pertinent? What, if anything, should I or could I do about it?

— Edgar Dale

He had read the "literature" of Dante before he read Dante, and he laughed as he recalled the pedantry with which he had known "all about" writers before he knew the writings of the writers themselves.

— Van Wyck Brooks

I sympathize with my youthful neighbor, who is struggling to inject a little order, a little taste and style, — a little readability, in short, — into a mass of manuscript that is supposed to be a book.

— Van Wyck Brooks

Every reader reads himself. The writer's work is merely a kind of optical instrument that makes it possible for the reader to discern what, without this book, he would perhaps never have seen in himself.

— Marcel Proust

Snoopy announces that he intends to read Tolstoy's epic novel, *War and Peace*, one word at a time. When Linus questions his pace, Snoopy replies, "I'm in no hurry. Besides, I like to think about what I read."

Let us assume that entertainment is the sole end of reading; even so, I think you would hold that no mental employment is so broadening to the sympathies or so enlightening to the understanding. Other pursuits belong not to all times, all ages, all conditions; but this gives stimulus to our youth and diversion to our old age; this adds a charm to success, and offers a haven of consolation to failure. Through the night-watches, on all our journeyings, and in our hours of ease, it is our unfailing companion.

— Cicero

Have you ever rightly considered what the mere ability to read means? That it is the key which admits us to the whole world of thought and fancy and imagination? to the company of saint and saga, of the wisest and the wittiest at their wisest and wittiest moment? That it enables us to see with the keenest eyes, hear with the finest ears, and listen to the sweetest voices of all time?

— James Russell Lowell

Free men read what they wish and freely discuss their reading with others. They know that you cannot get good answers unless you first have good questions. They are willing to tolerate ambiguity and uncertainty, knowing that the man who thinks he is absolutely right on complicated issues of the day is either naive, or totalitarian, or both.

—Edgar Dale

The uncritical reader often reads to erase experience. The critical reader tries to make a mentally indelible record of what he has read.

—Edgar Dale

In general, beyond the third grade level, the pupil who does not understand a statement which he attempts to read does not understand that statement when it is read or spoken to him. Furthermore, available data show that most pupils at intermediate and upper grade levels have as much difficulty in understanding the instructional talking of the teacher as they have in understanding what their textbooks say.

—Paul McKee

By the time a man can read a woman like a book, he's too old to start a library.

The critical reader knows that in dealing with great issues you can't really divide people into the good guys and the bad guys, the cops and the robbers, the saints and the sinners. You must learn to face both ambiguity and complexity.

—Edgar Dale

Responsibility

The person who is searching for responsibility will always find it.

Each of us is responsible for everything and to every human being.
— Fyodor Dostoyevsky

Bundles of wheat are not heavy if they're your own.
— Edgar Dale

You have to pay your dues if you wish to belong to the society in which you live.

Responsibility is the price every man must pay for freedom.
— Edith Hamilton

To grow into humanity, children and young people need increasing responsibility. To develop humane, compassionate people we must do fewer things *for* them and more things *with* them. We must help them earn their life.
— Edgar Dale

Science

The science of one age becomes the superstition of the next.
— George Lyman Kittredge

Science is a body of techniques of deduction and observation so organized that only one trained in these techniques will come to the same conclusions from the same assumptions *independently*.

Science lives on faith. We have talked much nonsense in our day about science's dealing only with what can be proved. Every scientific theory is a leap of faith, a gamble, and the so-called laws of science are generalities based on a certain number of experiments and hardly ever final. When it comes to the ultimate nature of the universe, science, like everything else, has to move out beyond the facts.
— Bishop Gerald Kennedy

We believe that the following values underlie science:
1. Longing to know and to understand
2. Questioning of all things
3. Search for data and their meaning
4. Demand for verification
5. Respect for logic
6. Consideration of premises
7. Consideration of consequences
— Educational Policies
Commission, 1966

Definition of science: "the attempt to find in the complexity of nature something which is simple and beautiful."
— Jacob Bronowski

Science is no more a collection of facts than a house is a collection of bricks.
— Jules Henri Poincaré

Speaking

Recipe for good speeches: Add shortening.

Rules for speaking: Stand up. Speak up. Shut up.

Public Speaking —
To make a speech successful, he
Devised a sure-fire recipe —
It's not the anecdotes and wit,
But the shortening he puts into it.
                    —Leonard K. Schiff

He had a knack of saying nothing fluently.

No preacher worth hearing will ever leave the impression that he is hurrying through a sermon as something that he is anxious to have done; rather, he should always leave people with the feeling that he had much more to say, that it is worth coming back to hear him further.
                    —The Very Reverend Ignatius
                        Smith

A conversationalist is one who can tell twice as many details as anybody wants to hear.

Professor X has a slight speech impediment. Every now and then he stops to breathe.

Look to your speech, lest it mar your fortune.
                    —William Shakespeare

While reading may often speak to the mind, it is through speech that the heart most often speaks to the heart. The heart will understand today what the mind understands tomorrow.

— James Stevens

The longer the spoke, the greater the tire.

If you don't strike oil in the first ten minutes, stop boring.

A speech should be as long as a piece of string — long enough to wrap up the package.

He had nothing to say and said it endlessly.

He was the kind of after-dinner speaker who was after dinner.

A poor speaker quits talking when he is tired. A good speaker quits before the audience is tired.

Before I start speaking I'd like to say something.

I can't speak Spanish today. My throat is so sore I can hardly speak English.

Sign on speaker's rostrum: "Caution: Engage Brain Before Starting Mouth."

Socrates said to a young man who was introduced to him to have his capabilities tested: "Talk in order that I may see you."

I love finished speakers
I mean I really do
I don't mean one that's polished
I mean one who's through.

He speaks 150 words a minute with gusts up to 200.

It's all right to hold a conversation but you should let go of it now and then.

— Richard Armour

Where ideas are lacking, words come to the rescue.
— Goethe

The speech was dull and unfortunately the speaker enunciated clearly.

College student to professor: "I liked the way you spoke. It was so fluent and decomposed."

Is there a line to be drawn anywhere when it comes to expression of opinion? Of course there is, but we must define it carefully. The line should be drawn at the point where words contribute directly to violation of law or to violence. In short, my right to swing my arm ends where the other fellow's nose begins.

— Arthur Garfield Hays

Success

How a man feels about himself is often more critical to his success than what he is objectively.
> — Harry Levinson, M.D.

When success turns a person's head, he is facing failure.
> — *Milwaukee Newman Club Bulletin*

Every man has one thing he can do better than anyone else — and usually it's reading his own handwriting.
> — G. Norman Collie

The key to success, according to today's youth, is the one that fits the ignition.
> — *Wall Street Journal*

His objective was not to be successful but to see how long he could postpone failure.

The successful man has a wife who tells him what to do and a secretary to do it.

Success is the best kind of motivation.

One of the advantages of success is that everybody stops giving you good advice.
> — Bernard Buffet

One way to be a success — give new names to old things.

The job of the college president is to push the professors without getting caught at it.

You need a track record before people are willing to bet on you.

A little boy was asked how he learned to skate. He replied: "Oh, by getting up every time I fell down."
> —Royal Bank of Canada
> *Monthly Letter*, January 1971

I think and think for months and years. Ninety-nine times the conclusion is false. The hundredth time I am right.
> —Albert Einstein

He aimed for happiness but settled for success.

If you can do it, it ain't brag.
> —Dizzy Dean

Teaching

Definition of the essence of teaching: "It is a matter of getting little fires started. And how to do it? What is required, sir, is to have a fire in the belly."
— Thomas Carlyle

Men must be taught as if you taught them not,
And things unknown proposed as things forgot.
— Alexander Pope

If a doctor, lawyer, or dentist had 40 people in his office at one time, all of whom had different needs, and some of whom didn't want to be there and were causing trouble, and the doctor, lawyer, or dentist, without assistance, had to treat them all with professional excellence for nine months, then he might have some conception of the classroom teacher's job.
— Donald D. Quinn

Don't mold, guide.

There are dull teachers, dull textbooks, dull films; but no dull subjects.

Comenius once wrote that his object was "to seek and find a method by which the teachers teach less and learners learn more."

To teach is to help someone learn something more quickly than he would learn it by trial and error.

A person who wants to learn will always find a teacher.
— Persian proverb

Teach as though you were teaching your own children.

A fine teacher is often one degree removed from a Ph.D.

Well thought is well-taught.

Practice what you teach.

You can't teach a child unless you reach him.

The young man taught all he knew and more;
The middle-aged man taught all he knew;
The old man taught all that his students could understand.
— Arnold Ross

The teacher, whether mother, priest, or schoolmaster, is the real maker of history.
— H. G. Wells

Teaching is truth mediated by personality.
— Phyllis Brooks

We can teach so that our students feel inferior, or so as to help them think better of themselves.

The teacher of English must no longer see himself as a custodian of a correctional institution, as a person who enforces subtle and dubious distinctions in word usage. Rather he thinks of himself not as a guard but as a guide, not as a suspicious watchman but as a creative explorer of language, an adventurer in ideas, as a communication facilitator.

The key question for all of us concerned with language is this: Are we enhancing and improving the free flow of ideas in our classroom and outside of it? Are we increasing mutuality, friendly association? Are we giving boys and girls, young men and young women an opportunity to associate with and to develop a zest for excellence?
— Edgar Dale

The greatest educational dogma is also its greatest fallacy: the belief that what must be learned can necessarily be taught.
—Sydney J. Harris

The task of a teacher is to help students become their own teachers.

To be a teacher in the right sense is to be a learner. I am not a teacher, only a fellow student.
—Sören Kierkegaard

Teachers of the past were skilled in handling words. The teachers of the future must be skilled in handling experiences.
—Edgar Dale

No man can be a good teacher unless he has feelings of warm affection toward his pupils and a genuine desire to impart to them what he himself believes to be of value.
—Bertrand Russell

Don't try to teach all you know. It may satisfy you but not the student.
—Edgar Dale

To teach is to transform by informing, to develop a zest for lifelong learning, to help pupils become students — mature independent learners, architects of an exciting, challenging future. Teaching at its best is a kind of communion, a meeting and merging of minds.
—Edgar Dale

Let the teacher make his charge pass everything through a sieve and lodge nothing in his head on mere authority or trust. . . . Let the student be asked for an account not merely of the words of his lesson, but of its sense and substance. . . . Let him be made to show what he has just learned in a hundred aspects, to see if he has made it his own.
—Montaigne

Technology

Technology is the most subtle and the most effective engineer of enduring social change. Its apparent neutrality is deceptive and often disarming.
— Robert MacIver

A technician is a man who understands everything about his job except its ultimate purpose and its place in the order of the universe.
— Sir Richard Livingston

Technology is not about tools, it deals with how Man works.
— Peter Drucker

Thinking

Everyone complains of his memory but no one of his judgment.

— La Rochefoucauld

Bernard Baruch has defined management thinking in terms of three basic parts: "thinking ahead, thinking through, and thinking whole."

Nothing ages people like not thinking.

— Christopher Morley

Definition of a sound thinker: One whose opinions coincide with our own.

When a little boy, I used to think that if I really had anything to tell I could make myself understood; and I think so still. The longer I live the surer I am that the chief difficulty of writers and speakers is the lack of interesting thoughts, and not of proper words.

When Darwin, one of the most honest of scientific thinkers, was speculating about the origin of species, he used to keep special notebooks in which he would immediately write down any objection to his theories which occurred to him. He found that, if he did not do this, his mind had a habit of forgetting all the objections. For the objections introduced disharmony into his mind; and his mind pushed them out again as quickly as possible.

— B. A. Howard

You can't delegate your thinking.

Many a man fails to become a thinker for the sole reason that his memory is too good.
— Nietzsche

As soon as you can say what you think, and not what some other person has thought for you, you are on the way to being a remarkable man.
— Sir James M. Barrie

Think things, not words.
— Oliver Wendell Holmes

Thinking is untidy. It is not either/or, black or white, but rather maybe, or sometimes, or possibly.
— Edgar Dale

Some flabby persons try to make education painless. "Do not," they say, "ask students to learn facts, but teach them to think." O Thinking — what intellectual crimes are committed in thy name! How can a man think if he doesn't know? Charles Darwin gathered biological facts for twenty years without seeing any binding relationship. Then one day, when he was walking through an English country lane, the idea of evolution suddenly came to him. That's what thinking is — the flashing emergence of an idea after facts have been mulled over a long time. Even then it is probably wrong. It must be well tested. Roentgen, the discoverer of X-rays, when asked what he thought they were, replied, 'I do not think; I experiment.' Thinking is a highly dangerous performance for amateurs; you cannot think with hopes and fears and ignorance, but only with a well-trained and well-filled mind.
— W. E. McNeill

To most people nothing is more troublesome than the effort of thinking.
— Sir James Bryce

A man who does not think for himself does not think at all.

If you make people think they're thinking, they'll love you. If you really make them think, they'll hate you.
— Don Marquis

Mind is the great lever of all thinking; human thought is the process by which all human ends are ultimately answered.
— Daniel Webster

Many people turn to television because they want to occupy time without occupying their minds.
— Edgar Dale

All our dignity lies in thought. By thought we must elevate ourselves, not by space and time which we cannot fill. Let us endeavor then to think well; therein lies the principle of morality.
— Blaise Pascal

What he lacked in depth he made up in shallowness.

The acquiring mind or the inquiring mind? We have a choice.

Nearly everybody thinks less than he knows and knows more than he thinks.

Thinking is talking to yourself and following certain rules for doing so.
— Edgar Dale

Few people think more than two or three times a year. I have made an international reputation for myself thinking once or twice a week.
— George Bernard Shaw

He was uncertain when he should have been certain, and he was certain when he should have been uncertain.

The wise man or woman makes many educated guesses.

The good mind has extra-sensitive perception.

He had only one mental file in which he put his information. It was labeled: Miscellaneous.

A good mind makes order out of clutter.
—Edgar Dale

He had no train of thought, just an ill-assorted string of box-cars.
—Edgar Dale

Time

As we advance in life, we acquire a keener sense of the value of time. Nothing else, indeed, seems of any consequence; and we become misers in this respect.

—William Hazlitt

His "cure" for everything — Time will take care of it.

—Edgar Dale

Let every man be master of his time
Till seven at night.

—William Shakespeare

What are we doing with all the time we save with these time-saving devices?

Why is it that the person who always says time is money never has any time?

Invest your precious time and money to get greatest returns.

. . . this time, like all times, is a very good one, if we but know what to do with it.

—Ralph Waldo Emerson

There are two things that have to happen before an idea catches on. One is that the idea should be good. The other is that it should fit in with the temper of the age. If it does not, even a good idea may well be passed by.

—Jawaharlal Nehru

I would rather be ashes than dust! I would rather that my spark should burn out in a brilliant blaze than it should be stifled by dry rot. I would rather be a superb meteor, every atom of me in magnificent flow, than a sleepy and permanent planet. The proper function of man is to live, not to exist. I shall not waste my days in trying to prolong them. I shall use my time.
                              — Jack London

Time is the most valuable thing that a man can spend.
                              — Diogenes

At times the whole world seems to be in conspiracy to importune you with emphatic trifles.
                              — Ralph Waldo Emerson

Act as though we didn't have all the time in the world.

Many people suffer from what might be called a mental pause. They forget to remember.

Truth

A man must have a good deal of vanity who believes, and a good deal of boldness who affirms, that all the doctrines he holds are true, and all he rejects are false.
> —Benjamin Franklin

No man is so thoroughly right as to be entitled to say that others are totally wrong. It is well to affirm your own truth, but it is not well to condemn those who think differently.
> —Socrates

The liar's punishment is not in the least that he is not believed, but that he cannot believe anyone else.
> —George Bernard Shaw

In one of Aesop's *Fables* he tells how Jupiter, in a mischievous mood, made mankind a present of spectacles. Every man had a pair, but they did not represent objects to all mankind alike. One pair was purple, another blue; one white and another grey; some were red, green and yellow. "However, notwithstanding this diversity," says Aesop, "every man was charmed with his own, believing it the best, and enjoyed in opinion all the satisfactions of truth."
> —The Royal Bank of Canada
> *Monthly Letter*, August 1977

Most of the great evils that man has inflicted upon man have come through people feeling quite certain about something which, in fact, was false.
> —Bertrand Russell

When in doubt, tell the truth.

—Mark Twain

No matter how seemingly unconnected with human affairs or remote from human interests a newly discovered truth may appear to be, time and genius will some day make it minister to human welfare.

—Robert Straker

Values

In the conditions of modern life the rule is absolute: The race which does not value trained intelligence is doomed. Not all your heroism, not all your social charm, not all your wit, not all your victories on land and sea, can move back the finger of fate.
— Alfred North Whitehead

What we obtain too cheaply we esteem too lightly; it is dearness only that gives everything its value.
— Thomas Paine

American philosopher, W. P. Montague . . . claims there's one simple question you and I must answer for ourselves before we'll be able to make any sense or any profit at life's strange rates of exchange. This question "Are the things that matter most finally at the mercy of the things that matter least?"
— Frederick Bruce Speakman

Her chief interest was not the cosmos but cosmetics.

Does not man, perhaps, love something besides well-being? Perhaps he is just as fond of suffering? Perhaps suffering is just as great a benefit to him as well-being?
— Fyodor Dostoyevsky

It is better to be a human being dissatisfied than a pig satisfied; better to be Socrates dissatisfied than a fool satisfied.
— John Stuart Mill

Today we have the money to do what we always said we wanted to do, but will we do it?

The aim of life is to spend it for something that will outlast it.
— William James

No longer talk at all about the kind of man that a good man ought to be, but be that man.
— Marcus Aurelius

A man does what he must — in spite of personal consequences, in spite of obstacles, and dangers, and pressures — and that is the basis of all human morality.
— John F. Kennedy

The overexamined life is not worth living.
— Edgar Dale

Always do right. This will gratify some people, and astonish the rest.
— Mark Twain

If it is better to travel than to arrive, it is because traveling is a constant arriving, while arrival that precludes further traveling is most easily attained by going to sleep or dying.
— John Dewey

Integrity without knowledge is weak and useless, . . . Knowledge without integrity is dangerous and dreadful.
— Samuel Johnson

We have the highest standard of low living in all history.
— Herbert J. Muller

I'm not really interested in being first, but I hate to be second.

There is something basically vulgar and banal about a society whose key entertainment — television — is preoccupied with headaches, digestive upsets, cigarettes, toiletries which make you smell good, non-abrasive toilet tissue, sexy automobiles.
— Edgar Dale

If you are right, be imperative.

If you have built castles in the air, your work need not be lost; that is where they should be. Now put foundations under them.

—Henry David Thoreau

Man's inhumanity to man
Makes countless thousands mourn!

—Robert Burns

Man is the only animal that laughs and weeps; for he is the only animal that is struck with the difference between what things are, and what they ought to be.

—William Hazlitt

I decline to accept the end of man . . . I believe that man will not merely endure: he will prevail. He is immortal not because he alone among creatures has an inexhaustible voice but because he has a soul, a spirit capable of compassion and sacrifice and endurance.

—William Faulkner

A State which dwarfs its men, in order that they may be more docile instruments in its hands even for beneficial purposes — will find that with small men no great thing can really be accomplished.

—John Stuart Mill

The heart has its reasons which reason knows nothing of.

—Blaise Pascal

Where the willingness is great, the difficulties cannot be great.

—Niccolo Machiavelli

A kind deed receives compound interest

The world is too much with us, late and soon,
Getting and spending, we lay waste our powers,
Little we see in nature that is ours
We have given our hearts away — a sordid boon.

—William Wordsworth

For both the individual and the nation, what should be most dreaded is not the loss of power but the loss of feeling. What is happening today is that the entire society is undergoing a decline in sensitivity — sensitivity to brutality, sensitivity to beauty, sensitivity to the possibilities of deeper living.
                    —Norman Cousins

Preserve the best and improve the rest. Instead of breaking the rules, first try to improve them.

The dilemma of any statesman is that he can never be certain about the probable course of events. In reaching a decision, he must inevitably act on the basis of an intuition that is inherently unprovable. If he insists on certainty, he runs the danger of becoming a prisoner of events. His resolution must reside not in "facts" as commonly conceived but in his vision of the future.
                    —Henry A. Kissinger

I don't believe in God but He has certainly been good to me.

Excessive and inflated advertising claims are more "subversive" of the capitalistic system than any amount of radical propaganda — and more effective, too, in creating cynics and unbelievers out of young children who quickly learn to distrust Establishment voices.

Make no little plans; they have no magic to stir men's blood and probably themselves will not be realized. Make big plans; aim high in hope and work, remembering that a noble, logical diagram once recorded will never die, but long after we are gone will be a living thing, asserting itself with ever-growing insistency. Remember that our sons and grandsons are going to do things that would stagger us. Let your watchword be order and your beacon beauty.
                    —Daniel H. Burnham

The moral issues of the modern world are embedded in the complex substance of science and technology. The greatest moral crime of our time is the concealment of the nature of nuclear war.
                    —Barry Commoner

The main trouble with despair is that it is self-fulfilling. People who fear the worst tend to invite it.

I believe that our Heavenly Father invented man because he was disappointed in the monkey.
—Mark Twain

If I were asked to what the singular prosperity and growing strength of the Americans ought to be attributed, I should reply: To the superiority of their women!
—Alexis de Tocqueville

Fashion is a form of ugliness so intolerable that we have to alter it every six months.
—Sydney Harris

Nobody should listen to a man giving a lecture or a sermon on his "philosophy of life" until we know exactly how he treats his wife, his children, his neighbors, his friends, his subordinates — and his enemies.
—Sydney Harris

Those who try too desperately to protect themselves from hurt are in the long run more vulnerable to injury; it is the hand that has developed calluses that slides more easily down the escape rope in an emergency.
—Sydney Harris

Don't waste your time in carping, disliking, griping, envying, resenting, hating, hurting. All the dividends you receive will be to get it all back in kind . . . so there is no gain. However, if you return love for hate, it will be the right thing to do and besides, it will make your critic feel cheap.
—Edgar Dale

There are a thousand hacking at the branches of evil to one who is striking at the root.
—Henry David Thoreau

The bad, the wrong often speaks with an amplified voice; the good may be voiceless, silent.
—Edgar Dale

Advice from Satchell Paige:
Avoid fried meat which angry up the blood.
If your stomach disputes you, lie down and pacify it with cool thoughts.
Keep the juices flowing by jangling around gently as you move.
Go lightly on the vices such as carrying on in society.
Avoid running at all times.
Don't look back. Something might be gaining on you.

If you don't care for slum children while you are worrying about bald eagles, well, you are just getting your priorities a bit wrong.

—Barbara Ward

It is lack of confidence, more than anything else, that kills a civilization. We can destroy ourselves.

—Kenneth Clark

As long as you live, keep learning how to live.

—Seneca

He didn't lose much. All he lost was his meager self-respect.

What are you for? You keep telling me what you are against. But what are you for? What do you prize? Or do you assume a kind of sophisticated irresponsibility — a kind of amused spectatorship?

—Edgar Dale

Vocabulary

The apprentice learns to use words as he learns to use other tools and materials, by working side by side with the craftsman.

Your vocabulary is mean and impoverished; but quite adequate to express your thoughts.
— Griff Niblack

The knowledge of words is the gate to scholarship.
— Woodrow Wilson

Seriously, our learned persons and possessors of special information should not, when they are writing for the general public, presume to improve the accepted vocabulary. When they are addressing audiences of their likes, they may naturally use, to their hearts' content, the forms that are most familiar to writer and readers alike; but otherwise they should be at pains to translate technical terms into English. And, what is of far greater importance, when they do forget this duty, we others who are unlearned, and naturally speak not in technical terms but in English, should refuse to be either cowed by the fear of seeming ignorant, or tempted by the hope of passing for specialists, into following their bad example without their real though insufficient excuse.
— Margaret Nicholson

The purpose of a big vocabulary is not to use all of the words but to be discriminating in the choice of those selected to be used or discarded.

Words must do more than fit the sense. They must, also, please the ear; for in prose as well as verse there is a kind of cadence, although of a different and more liberal sort.

Words, words, mere words, no matter from the heart.
— William Shakespeare

We should have a great many fewer disputes in the world if words were taken for what they are, the signs of our ideas only, and not for things themselves.
— John Locke

Words are like leaves, and where they most abound,
Much fruit of sense beneath is rarely found.
— Alexander Pope

Among the English language's many puzzling words is "economy," which means the large size in soap flakes and the small size in automobiles.
— *The Alcoa News*

A powerful agent is the right word. Whenever we come upon one of these intensely right words in a book or newspaper the resulting effect is physical as well as spiritual, and electrifyingly prompt.
— Mark Twain

His speech was neither rare nor well done.

Big words may cover up little thoughts.

There are masked words abroad, I say, which nobody understands.
— John Ruskin

. . . except ye utter by the tongue words easy to be understood, how shall it be known what is spoken? For ye shall speak into the air.
— I Corinthians 14:9

Irreverence is another man's disrespect for your god. There isn't any word that tells what your disrespect for his god is.
— Mark Twain

We all declare for liberty; but in using the same word we do not all mean the same thing. With some the word liberty may mean for each man to do as he pleases with himself . . . while with others the same word may mean for some men to do as they please with other men. . .

—Abraham Lincoln

Every word has a history and buried deep in the meaning of words lies the story of our civilization. To know words well is to know where we have been and to forecast where we are going.

—Edgar Dale

Small children know more than they can say. Adults say more than they know.

Diminish vocabulary and you diminish life.

People who live circumscribed lives have circumscribed vocabulary.

Abuse of words has been the great instrument of sophistry and chicanery, of party, faction, and division of society.

—John Adams

Words are what hold society together.

—Stuart Chase

Give me the right word and the right accent and I will move the world.

—Joseph Conrad

In our Victorian dislike of the practice of calling a spade a bloody shovel, it is not necessary to go to the opposite extreme of calling it an agricultural implement.

—Robert W. Seton-Watson

Words are not mere. Words are the deposit of rich experiences. They inform, they challenge, they amplify, they document, distill the wisdom of the past. They signal the kind of life the individual has lived. Has it been mean, meager?

—Edgar Dale

With words we govern men.
— Benjamin Disraeli

When a teacher calls a boy by his entire name it means trouble.
— Mark Twain

To fully exercise wordmanship we use such terms as aegis, facet, corpus, posture, arcane, paradigm, ancillary, scenario. For the next higher level, use words like chiliastic, Manichean, parameter.
— Edgar Dale

At the lower levels of reading you pronounce words you don't know. At the higher levels of reading you know words you can't pronounce.

Nothing, surely, is more alive than a word.
— J. Donald Adams

"I pledge thee my troth." I used to feel that was awfully stilted until I found out the meaning of the word "troth." Did you know that it means "a promise with long range implications?" I've felt good about that word ever since.
— Howard L. Huntzicker

A sensitivity to words, a breadth and depth of vocabulary, an ability to analyze words in sentences, are all characteristics of what we would call the educated man.
— Edgar Dale

Writing

To write well you must sometimes say well what individuals believe but cannot express. You must also say the unexpected in such a way that the reader says, "you know, he's got something there" . . . the unexpected delights, the serendipities.
— Edgar Dale

No passion in the world, no love or hate, is equal to the passion to alter someone else's draft.
— H. G. Wells

Polyverbosity . . . is a common disease of seniors and young instructors, and of some professors also. It should be repressed and sternly. Once a student can be persuaded that the best writing is usually the briefest . . . [he learns] that his "yes" must be "yes" and not semantic affirmation.
— G. G. Harrison

Poets are born, not made, but the ability is given to every man of average intelligence to write clear, orderly prose.
— Herbert Read

Definition of good prose: It must satisfy the intellect which asks primarily for "intelligibility — for clearness; it wishes no more; and it lays stress on beauty of language only as this may promote clearness and lighten the task of understanding."
— Wackernagel

Don't be more precise than the subject warrants.
— Plato

The interest of the professor is to become more unassailable, and so more authoritative. He achieves this by becoming more technical. For the more technical he gets, the fewer can comprehend him; the fewer are competent to criticize him, the more of an oracle he becomes; if, therefore, he wishes for an easy life of undisturbed academic leisure, the more he will indulge his natural tendency to grow more technical as his knowledge grows, the more he will turn away from those aspects of his subject which have any direct practical or human interest.

—F. C. S. Schiller

Clarity begins at home

Good writing is disciplined talking.

—James Boswell

The greatest part of a writer's time is spent in reading; in order to write, a man will turn over half a library to make one book.

—James Boswell

Poor style in original means poor style in adaptation.

His writing is dull enough to be scholarly.

A child says, "Do it again"; a teacher says, "Repeat the exercise"; But the sociologist says, "It was determined to replicate the investigation."

The pen is the tongue of the mind.

—Cervantes

If you wish to become a writer, write.

—Epictetus

It is one test of a fully developed writer that he reminds us of no one but himself.

—Melvin Maddocks

Thurber did not write the way a surgeon operates, he wrote the way a child skips rope, the way a mouse waltzes.

—E. B. White

Vague enough to sound profound, precious enough to seem literary.

Most bad journalism is only high-brow verbosity, yet the popular mind continues to believe that the pedantry which it likes is simple and the simplicity which it finds hard is complex.

— Jacques Barzun

A poor writer lacks comma sense.

Napoleon wrote to one of his staff: "I have received your letter. I don't understand a word of it. I can't have explained myself clearly."

The good writer seems to be writing about himself but has his eye always on that thread of the universe which runs through himself, and all things.

— Ralph Waldo Emerson

The able writer satisfies our hunger for tangibility.

The article was too long. It should be reduced by three-thirds.

A writer thinks with his fingers. A speaker thinks with his tongue.

Simplify the vocabulary. Avoid pedantic mumbo-jumbo. You can sometimes substitute short, simple, vivid, easily understood words for the longer Latin or Greek equivalents. Instead of *confronting* problems, just face them. A *sine qua non* is merely a necessity. A *multi-faceted* problem is many-sided. A *unilateral* treaty is a one-sided treaty. Don't *proceed on the assumption*. Just *assume*.

— Edgar Dale

A first draft usually has a lot of wind in it.

— Edgar Dale

A lazy reader not only wants the writer to cut his wood but also to put it on the fire.

— Edgar Dale

A simple test of one's writing is: Is it tellable? Is there substance, or does the meaning vanish when you rephrase it for someone else?

Advice to graduate students: All work and no plagiarism makes dull writing.

There are only two hard things to write in a play — the first act and the third act. The second act will take care of itself.
— Moss Hart

Is it deep stuff or is it merely badly written?

Eschew prolix obfuscation.

His articles are harder to read than they are to write.
— Edgar Dale

An able writer re-reads his manuscript so that his reader won't have to.
— Edgar Dale

Writing is for reading. Better writing makes better reading, and better reading makes better writing.
— Edgar Dale

The writer gives ideals to his times. He gives people a sense that what is necessary is also possible. And out of the writer's ideals a society receives its basic energy. There has never been a great society without great writers.
— Norman Cousins

He was an expansive writer. He could take a clear, crisp sentence and make two muddy paragraphs out of it.

Our discussion will be adequate if it has as much clearness as the subject-matter admits of, for precision is not to be sought for alike in all discussions, any more than in all the products of the crafts. Now fine and just actions, which political science investigates, admit of much variety and fluctuation of opinion, so that they may be thought to exist only by convention and not by nature. . .
— Aristotle

Whatever you teach, be brief, that your readers' minds may readily comprehend and faithfully retain your words.
— Horace

If you are like Thoreau you will have learned how to keep your accounts on your thumb-nail. Simplicity, simplicity, simplicity!
— Reginald L. Cook

There is fear of simplicity lest one be thought simple; fear of clarity lest one be thought transparent; fear of lucidity lest one be thought glib. Along with this is the quaint but respectable notion that good scholarship requires academic jargon interlarded and overlarded — hence the love of the mouth-filling phrase and the worship of the polysyllables. Scholars have failed to build a bridge to the very public they are anxious to serve . . . they are apparently unaware that understanding is tied to communication.
— Norman Cousins

Literature is the art of writing something that will be read twice.
— Cyril Connolly

The source of bad writing is the desire to be something more than a man of sense — the straining to be thought a genius; and it is just the same in speech-making. If men would only say what they have to say in plain terms, how much more eloquent they would be!
— Samuel Taylor Coleridge